DISCOVERING

STEM at the
Airport

STEM in the Real World

Cynthia Roby

PowerKiDS press.

New York

Published in 2016 by The Rosen Publishing Group, Inc.
29 East 21st Street, New York, NY 10010

First Edition

Editor: Sarah Machajewski
Book Design: Mickey Harmon

Photo Credits: Cover (control room) Culutra RM/Koca Little Company/Collection Mix: Subjects/Getty Images; cover, pp. 1, 3–4, 6, 8, 10, 12, 14, 16, 18, 20, 22–24 (banner design) linagifts/Shutterstock.com; cover, pp. 1, 4, 6, 8, 14, 20 (logo/caption box) Vjom/Shutterstock.com; pp. 5, 22 michaeljung/Shutterstock.com; p. 7 Tupungato/Shutterstock.com; p. 9 FamVeld/Shutterstock.com; p. 11 Vladimirs Koskins/Shutterstock.com; p. 13 Baerbel Schmidt/Stone/Getty Images; p. 15 SIHASAKPRACHUM/Shutterstock.com; p. 16 Jaromir Chalabala/Shutterstock.com; p. 17 Sorbis/Shutterstock.com; p. 18 James Steidl/Shutterstock.com; p. 19 Monty Rakusen/Cultura/Getty Images; p. 21 Perfect Gui/Shutterstock.com.

Library of Congress Cataloging-in-Publication Data

Roby, Cynthia, author.
 Discovering STEM at the airport / Cynthia Roby.
    pages cm. — (STEM in the real world)
 Includes bibliographical references and index.
 ISBN 978-1-4994-0907-9 (pbk.)
 ISBN 978-1-4994-0908-6 (6 pack)
 ISBN 978-1-4994-0958-1 (library binding)
 1. Airports—Miscellanea—Juvenile literature. 2. Science—Study and teaching (Elementary)—Juvenile literature. I. Title.
 TL725.15.R63 2016
 387.7'36—dc23
                                        2015006134

Manufactured in the United States of America

CPSIA Compliance Information: Batch #WS15PK: For Further Information contact Rosen Publishing, New York, New York at 1-800-237-9932

Contents

Where Would You Go?

Family trips can be exciting. Where in the world would you like to go? You might want to see the ocean, go camping, or climb a mountain. Imagine these places are far away. How would you get there?

Taking an airplane is one way to travel. To get on a plane, you must go to the airport. While in the airport, you'll see lots of STEM. "STEM" stands for "science, **technology**, **engineering**, and math." Let's see how discovering STEM can make your family trip an exciting learning adventure!

Think of all the science, technology, engineering, and math that goes into making an airport—and planes—run smoothly.

STEM Smarts

While you're at the airport, see if you can spot STEM at work. Check your smartphone for more STEM facts.

Arriving at the Airport

Thousands of people pass through airports every day, but they can't all be there at the same time. Airlines use math, the M in STEM, to **schedule** flights in the best way possible.

Airline workers look at millions of data, or facts, when scheduling flights. The data tell them the number of travelers in a day and when most people are traveling. They use math equations to find out how many flights can leave or arrive at a certain time, how many people these flights can carry, and more.

Airlines never want to have too many or too few flights. That's where math comes in—airlines use data from past flights to know how to schedule flights in the future.

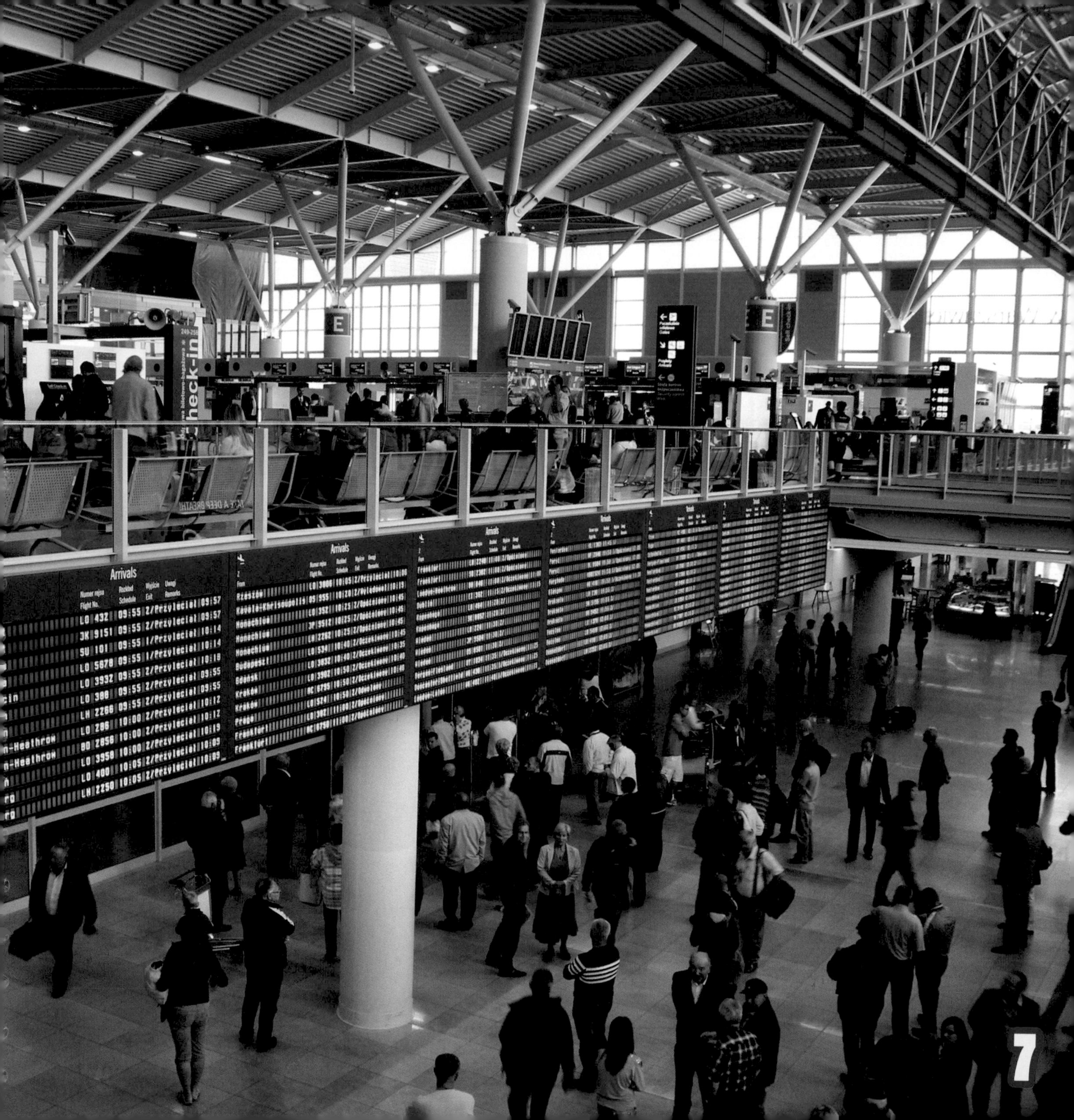
Arrivals
Arrivals
Arrivals
check-in
E
E

Getting Around

Getting around the airport is easy. Travelers can use moving stairs called escalators. Escalators are large, but the technology and engineering behind them is simple.

An escalator's steps are pulled by two **chains**. The chains are looped around gears. A **motor** turns the gears, and the gears turn the chains. The chains move the steps, which are engineered to always stay flat. This technology allows people to stand still and be carried between floors. They don't have to climb stairs while carrying heavy suitcases.

The engineers who created escalators helped make traveling easier. Escalators are also used in stores, libraries, office buildings, and other places.

STEM Smarts

Escalators move about 145 feet (44 m) per minute. They can carry more than 10,000 people an hour.

Checking Bags

People usually travel with a lot of baggage, or personal belongings packed into suitcases. Most of it is carried in the bottom part of the plane. Airports use computers to control how the bags are carried from check-in counters to the planes.

A computer prints out a tag for your suitcase. The tag is **coded** with the name of the place you're flying to. The baggage is then placed on a moving belt. Computer **scanners** read the tags as the bags move, and sorting machines send them to the right plane.

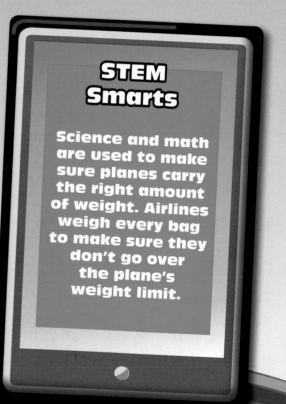

STEM Smarts

Science and math are used to make sure planes carry the right amount of weight. Airlines weigh every bag to make sure they don't go over the plane's weight limit.

These bags have been tagged and coded.
They're on their way to the airplane!

Airport Security

Every passenger, or traveler, who's going on a plane must first go through the airport's **security** checkpoint. This keeps everyone in the airport—and in the air—safe.

Security workers take every traveler's ticket and match it to their I.D., or official paper telling who someone is. Then, passengers take off their shoes, belt, and any other metal they may be wearing. Passengers step through a metal detector, which is a machine that uses an electric current to tell if someone has metal on them.

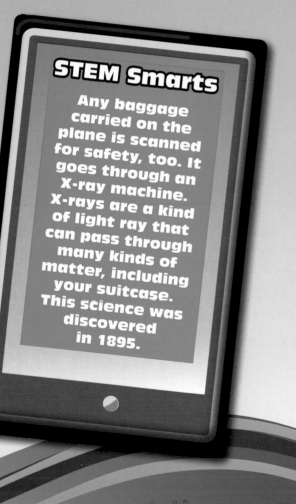

STEM Smarts

Any baggage carried on the plane is scanned for safety, too. It goes through an X-ray machine. X-rays are a kind of light ray that can pass through many kinds of matter, including your suitcase. This science was discovered in 1895.

You may be worried about stepping through a metal detector, but it won't harm your body. Scientists and engineers have figured out how to build machines that don't hurt us.

13

STEM Screens

Once passengers get through security, they can look at a big screen to see where their plane is and when it's leaving. The screen may say a flight is on time or that it's leaving later than they thought. This data comes from computers that track planes as they come and go and as they're in flight.

Travelers whose flights are late may use their math skills to see how much time has been added to their travel day. They may have enough time to get something to eat, or they may just wait at their gate.

Engineers use all their STEM skills to create screens such as the ones pictured here. This technology keeps passengers on time and tells them where their plane is.

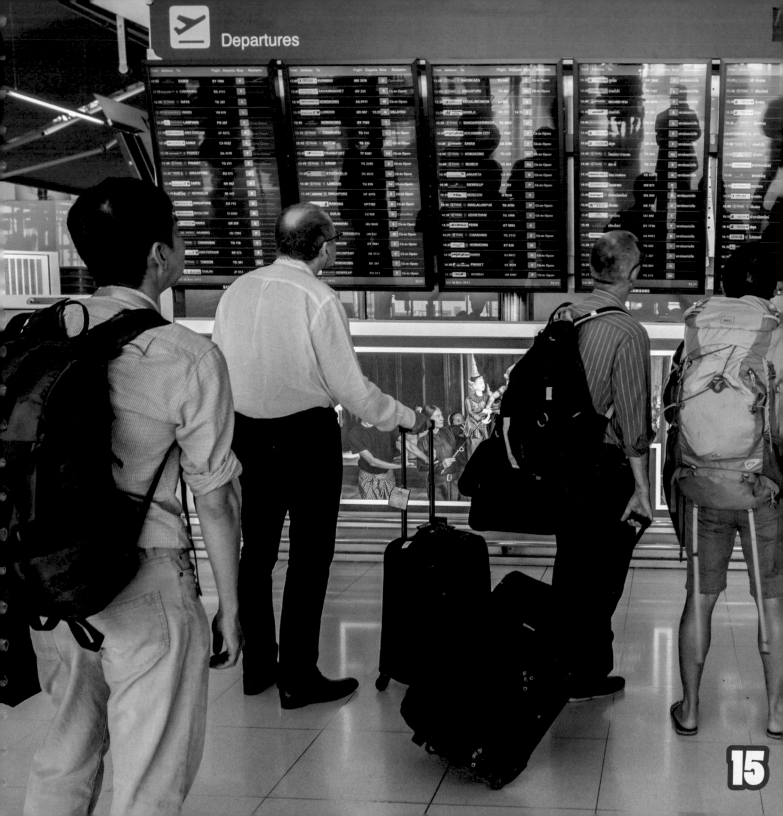

15

Preflight Check

Travelers board, or get on, the plane shortly before it leaves. Technology affects this part of a traveler's trip, too. An airline worker uses a microphone and a speaker to announce when boarding begins. People wait in line as a computer scans their ticket. Then, they find their seat.

Pilots carry out a preflight check before the plane takes off. They check the tools and controls both inside and outside the plane to make sure they're working. This can be as simple as making sure lights turn on and off.

STEM Smarts

Position lights show where a plane is in the air. Some lights flash to tell other planes where a plane is when it's hard to see. Landing lights lining the runway help pilots see where to land.

Pilots operate planes from the cockpit. It's full of high-tech tools such as computers, compasses, radios, and more.

Ready for Takeoff

Once the pilot finishes the preflight check, the plane is ready for takeoff! With so many airplanes on the runway at once, how does a plane leave the airport safely?

Every airport has a **traffic** control tower. Inside the tower, radios keep track of all the planes in the air. The people who work in these towers are called air traffic controllers. They use radar, a kind of technology, to make sure planes have enough clear space to take off and land safely.

Traffic control towers have tools that spin around and send radio waves into the air. When radio waves find and hit a plane, they travel back to the radar detector and tell workers where the plane is.

STEM Smarts

Some people inside the traffic control tower use their science skills to keep track of the weather. Bad weather such as wind, snow, or rain can lead to a lot of problems at an airport.

The Science of Flight

Takeoff might be the best part of flying. What keeps such a heavy machine in the air? STEM! Planes have come a long way since the first ones were invented more than 100 years ago, thanks to science and engineering.

Huge engines move the plane forward at a high **speed**. The air flows over and under the wings, and creates a force strong enough to lift the plane. This happens because the **air pressure** over the wing is less than the pressure under the wing.

Pilots must use all their STEM skills as they fly. Science helps them steer the plane, technology and engineering help control the plane's tools, and math keeps pilots on time and in the right place in the air.

STEM Smarts

Planes fly about 30,000 feet (9,124 m) in the air. People can't breathe at that height because the air pressure is too low. Planes pump high-pressure air into the seating area so people can breathe like they do on the ground.

Bon Voyage!

STEM is everywhere at the airport, but you don't have to get on a plane to find it. Some airports allow families or schools to take tours and see STEM at work. No matter what brings you to an airport, you're sure to see STEM all around you.

If you're taking an airplane trip, look for STEM when you get to where you're going. Watch closely for science, technology, engineering, and math at work. They're everywhere!

Glossary

air pressure: The force of molecules in the air pushing on each other.

chain: A series of connected metal links that pull and support loads.

code: To put into a system of words, letters, and numbers.

engineering: The use of science and math to improve our world.

motor: A machine powered by electricity that is used to power something else.

runway: A leveled strip of smooth ground along which aircraft take off and land.

scanner: A machine that passes a beam of light over an object in order to know what it is.

schedule: To plan things at certain times.

security: Actions taken to keep something safe.

speed: How fast something moves.

technology: The way people do something using tools and the tools that they use.

traffic: The transportation of people or goods.

Index

Websites

Due to the changing nature of Internet links, PowerKids Press has developed an online list of websites related to the subject of this book. This site is updated regularly. Please use this link to access the list: www.powerkidslinks.com/stem/airp